Training Manual

Leading God's People

Published by Hadassah's Crown, LLC
Simpsonville, SC 29681

Text Copyright © 2018 by Rudolph Burdett, Jr.

All rights reserved. No part of this book may be reproduced, scanned, or distributed in any printed or electronic form or by any means without prior written consent of the publisher, except for brief quotes used in reviews.

Please do not participate in or encourage piracy of copyrighted materials in violation of the author's rights. Purchase only authorized editions.

All scripture quotations, unless otherwise indicated, are taken from The King James Bible Second Edition ©1984, 1990, 2008 by AMG International, Inc; and The New Unger's Bible Dictionary Original Work Copyright © 1957 The Moody Bible Institute of Chicago, Revised Edition © 1961, 1966 The Moody Bible Institute of Chicago, Copyright Renewed 1985 by Pearl C. Unger, Revised and Updated Edition 1988 Addition and New Material Copyright © 1988 The Moody Bible Institute of Chicago.

Library of Congress Control Number: 2018949425
Printed in the United States
ISBN 978-0-9981230-6-6

www.hadassahscrownpublishing.com

Introduction

Leading God's people has never been easy, from Moses leading the children of Israel even to us allowing the Lord to lead us today through His Word.

Jesus chose unlearned and untrained disciples before they made an impact on the world and led the world to Christ. You may not have a bunch of letters behind your name. In other words, you may not be educated. You can still impact this world for Christ

Moses, Jeremiah and Gideon used excuses before they led God's people. The point is, when God calls you, don't use excuses.

David was a shepherd boy. Peter messed up and began to sink. Paul persecuted Christians. Daniel took a stand. Ezekiel answered God's call. All leaders were not born leaders; they were trained or taught how to lead.

This training manual is designed to prepare servants in various capacities and help individuals in leading others.

The objective of training people to serve in various capacities is not to criticize, embarrass or to make fun of anyone. This manual is designed to increase learning and to enhance our skills in better serving the Lord and leading God's people.

People should be taught and trained how to present their best. People should also be trained in leadership. Leaders should be taught to encourage others and to not hinder them.

This manual also discusses Christian leaders. This manual is to enhance leadership skills, in spite of age, gender, marital status, or occupation, for the glory of God.

Romans 15:4 says, "For whatsoever things were written aforetime were written for our learning, that we through patience and comfort of the scriptures might have hope."

As you look at people of God and answer the questions in this study, I pray you will look at yourself to make sure you are being all that God has called you to be.

Table of Contents

Lesson 1……………....………………….Public Prayer

Lesson 2……………..………...…….….Announcements

Lesson 3…………………………..………Public Speaking

Lesson 4……………………….…………Scripture Reading

Lesson 5……………………………The Lord's Supper

Lesson 6……...………………Consider Leading Through
The Ministry of Music………....…Song Leading

Lesson 7……..……………………………………Offering

Lesson 8…….………………Responding to Responses

Lesson 9……..……………………………………Ushering

Lesson 10……...……………………………………Baptizing

Lesson 11……………………………………...Teaching

Lesson 12……………………………………....Moses

Lesson 13……………………………………...Joshua

Lesson 14……………………………………..Gideon

Lesson 15……………………………………David

Lesson 16……………………………………Elijah

Lesson 17……………………………………………Solomon

Lesson 18…….……………………………………....Isaiah

Lesson 19……………………………………...Jeremiah

Lesson 20…………………………………………..Ezekiel

Lesson 21……………………………………………Daniel

Lesson 22…………………………………….Jesus Christ

Lesson 23……………………………………………...Paul

Lesson 24……………………………………………..Peter

Getting Acquainted

You will be surprised how little you know about other members in class. Most of the time, we speak in passing and we say we know the person. Start out by telling the class a little about yourself. If possible, answer the following questions:

1. What is your full name?
2. Do you have a nickname? If you do, what is it?
3. What are your hobbies?
4. Do you have a family? If so, what are their names?
5. What's your favorite color?
6. Do you like to watch or play sports?
7. Where is your residence?
8. Do you have an objective for this class?
9. Discuss miscellaneous items, such as class expectations.

Try to relax and be comfortable. Most people like to talk about themselves. You will see making a speech by standing in front of someone is not complex when you are comfortable with your subject matter.

The number of people in the class will determine the amount of time used. Most often, a maximum of five minutes is used to discuss the above questions.

Please lead a song................. **assign someone**

Opening Pray..................………**assign someone**

Please make a five to ten-minute speech before or after class…………………………..**assign someone**

Be ready to critique. Not criticize.

Lesson 1
Public Prayer

Some of us treat God like a genie, individually and especially collectively, as a congregation. We make prayers (wishes) for others. If those prayers (wishes) are not answered the way we led the congregation in prayer, we are upset or even angry because God didn't answer the way we prayed.

The prayers (wishes) are not that God doesn't hear. It may not be answered because God is trying to teach the congregation something through experience.

Let's talk about the meaning of prayer. Prayer is petition, intercession, adoration, meditation, praise and thanksgiving to God. In simplest terms, prayer is actually talking to God. It's the avenue to the throne of God through Jesus Christ. Prayer is one of the most powerful resources known to mankind.

The best model prayer is found in Matthew 6:8-13. In this passage, Jesus's disciples asked Him to teach them how to pray. You will notice the following components of the model prayer:

1. The person addressed   2. The request for food
3. Forgiveness   4. Protection
5. Petition

Our prayers should end with "in Jesus' name." (Colossians 3:17; John 14:13-14). James 5:15-18 tells us that the prayer of faith by the effectual fervent prayer of a righteous man availeth much. Our public prayers, the first couple of words, can either put the congregation to sleep mentally or they will hang on to every word. I know, some may say it doesn't make a difference; you are praying to God. Yes, it does! We are leading God's people.

There are some perquisites concerning "Public Prayer." They are as follows:

1. The person must be a Christian. (John 9:31)
2. The person must believe in prayer. (James 1:6)
3. The person must desire that the will of God be done. (Matthew 26:39)

Those things that we consider important and life threatening require a trained professional.

- A doctor must be trained in his or her profession.
- A dentist must be trained in his or her profession.
- A DMV will at first require a teenager to drive with someone over 18 who is trained.
- A barber must be trained in his profession.
- A lawyer must be trained in his profession.

A person must be trained in leading public prayer. A person must realize that when he is praying publicly, it is no longer "I" but "we" and that person is leading the congregation in prayer.

When a person prays publicly or privately, there can be sentence prayers or chain prayers.

- Sentence prayers – Can be one or more sentences.

- Chain prayers - To pray for the needs and emergencies of our church family by contacting a person, then they contact someone, and on and on.

Do's
1. Be enthusiastic.
2. Speak loudly.
3. Be ready.
4. Be clear.
5. Have proper conduct and mannerism.
6. Closing prayers should be in Jesus' name.

Don'ts
7. Pray too long.
8. Avoid repetition.
9. Do it to be seen of men.

Matthew 6:5-7 says,

> "⁵And when thou prayest, thou shalt not be as the hypocrites are: for they love to pray standing in the synagogues and in the corners of the streets, that they may be seen of men. Verily, I say unto you, They have their reward.
>
> ⁶ But thou, when thou prayest, enter into thy closet, and when thou hast shut thy door, pray to thy Father which is in secret; and thy Father which seeth in secret shall reward thee openly.

> ⁷ But when ye pray, use not vain repetitions, as the heathen do: for they think that they shall be heard for their much speaking."

In these scriptures, I noticed Jesus mentioned two types of prayers. One was the "showcase prayer." This is where the person draws attention to themselves from others. The other is a "relational prayer." This is where the person seeks time with the Father.

Often, one of the greatest things to hinder us in public praying is fear. We feel fear will mess us up by causing us to stumble, lock-up, or become brain dead.

Many times, when we lead prayers, we lead them in front of people we know. I know sometimes we may go out of town, but that may be rare. Don't be scared. To better lead others in prayer, follow the steps below.

Pray for God's help.
> When you know in advance that you are going to lead God's people in a prayer, that is a plus. Pray ahead of time by asking God to help privily in this effort.

Resolve to pray.
> This is a great privilege and honor. Determine ahead of time you will pray aloud if given the opportunity.

Consider what you will pray.
> Think ahead of occasions like Thanksgiving, Christmas, other holidays, and/or birthdays. If someone is sick, unavailable, struggling with problems, etc., pray. Pray in a way that will allow others to be able to follow.

Consider how you will pray.
> In an humble, sincere way with faith and boldly, bring all things to God's throne.

Just pray.
> God is with you. There is intercession by the Spirit. God hears the prayers of the little children and faithful members, just pray.

In order to have an effective and efficient public prayer, we need to pray with faith both publicly and privately.

Prayer is not reduced to a ritual or a routine, like carrying a Bible or wearing a big cross; public prayer is leading God's people. Again, it is a great privilege and honor.

Listed below are prayers by Biblical prophets and individuals.

1. Matthew 26:39-42

2. I Samuel 1:11

3. II Samuel 12:16

4. Luke 11:11-12

5. Acts 12:12-14

Be ready to discuss the scriptures above.

Questions Regarding Public Prayer

1. What exactly is prayer?

2. Why is prayer so important?

3. Do I have to get on my knees or close my eyes to pray?

4. Are Christians required to pray?

5. Does an individual know their prayer is heard by God?

6. I've heard people pray the same prayer over and over. Is this acceptable to God?

7. Should a person pray more than once?

8. If a Christian prays in Mary's name, should they be corrected? When? How?

9. Why does God not answer some prayers by Christians and non-Christians?

10. Is prayer necessary for salvation?

11. Matthew 6:6 discusses praying in private. Is private prayer important?

12. Can social media platforms for prayer be effective?

Please lead a song................ **assign someone**

Opening Pray...........................**assign someone**

Please make five to ten-minute speech before or after class........................... **assign someone**

Be ready to critique. Not criticize.

Lesson 2
Announcements

The intent of announcements is to provide information to the congregation. The way information is communicated is very important. The information should be collected, compiled, condensed and reviewed beforehand by the person making announcements to effectively maximize time and to eliminate confusion.

Please critique the following announcement. Then, we will look at some steps to have more effective announcements.

> Example: It's time for announcements. I don't know where the folder is with the announcements in it. Oh! Here it is. Uh! Uh! There is a gospel meeting at the church of Christ in Rockville, MD next week. Uh! Uh! Let's see, Sister Mary is sick at the hospital. I don't know what's wrong with her, but she can walk now. I have a note here. Uh! Brother Brown is asking us to pray for his cousin Sam for some kind of treatment. I can't pronounce the word, but let's pray for him anyway. You know, when I was in school I was never good in English, but I was lucky enough to pass.

If you have a copy of the bulletin, please look on the back. There will be a fellowship meal at the Anywhere Church of Christ in Clinton, MD November 16.... There will be a Sing-Along at the Church of Christ in Annapolis, MD on October 8 ....

There is a game night at the Doe's resident September 1....

Did you see anything wrong with this announcement or anything that could be improved upon? If the answer is yes, please make the necessary changes and share with the class. Listed below are steps to assist in making effective announcements.

Be prepared to make announcements

It's good to assign someone before worship. This person's communication must be clear, concise, and articulate. Make sure all information is given ahead of time. It's also a good idea to read and go over announcements silently.

Prepare yourself.

Prepare yourself mentally. Read through the announcements to identify any errors and familiarize yourself with the information.

Acknowledge Your Guests.

Acknowledging your guests is something churches should do every Sunday. Let guests know they are appreciated and welcomed. Some call guests out via visitor cards, others ask them to raise their hands, and some ask them to stand and speak. Either way, make sure your guests are acknowledged.

Making Immediate Announcements.

Announcing everything will cause the congregation to not hear anything. It's good to announce the immediate (Things that will happen in the next week.) Again, it's not good to announce everything. Most of the time, 99% the announcements are located in the bulletin.

Do's
1. Project.
2. Speak audibly
3. Be brief.
4. Be clear.
5. Stand straight without moving excessively.

Don'ts
6. Mention everything.
7. Minimize any announcements.

Practice announcements:
1 – Ladies' Bible Class 7/3/18 held at the building Monday at 6:00pm.
2 – Brothers' Business Meeting July 03, 2018 held at the building at 8:00 am.
3 – Teachers' meeting the first Monday of each month at 5:00 pm.
4 – Teachers are needed.
5 – Sally Joe is at the Round Hospital in Room 303.

Practice announcements:
1 – Brothers' meeting 10:00 am on 6/18/18 at the building.
2 – Gospel meeting at the Anywhere Church of Christ in Knoxville, TN at 6/20-22/18 @ 7:30 pm
3 – Sick & Shut-in are as follows
4 – Brother John Doe will be traveling?

Practice announcements:
1- Students for adult class pick-up materials.

2- All ladies meet up front after worship.
3- All college students and young adults have a meeting on 7/21/18 @ 6:00 pm.

Practice announcements:
1- Elders' meeting on 7/7/18 at 6:00 pm at the building.
2- Ladies' meeting on 7/28/18 at 3:00 pm for organization of ladies' day.
3- Movie night at the Burdett's home on 6/30/18 @ 8:00 pm
4- Bowling night 6/23/18 @ 6:00 pm.
5- Sick &shut-in

Practice announcements:
1- Deacons meeting in conference room 04/08/18 @ 7:00 pm.
2- Sick & shut-in
3- Gospel meeting @ Maysville Church of Christ 4/4-7/18 @ 7:30 pm.
4- College students & young adults meet up front after service.

Practice announcements:
1- Ladies Bible class 5/7/18 held at the building at 6:00 pm.
2- Welcome visitors & guests.
3- 5th Sunday Fellowship will be at the Selma Congregation at 3:00 pm.
4- Brother John Doe is at Crown Hospital Room 202.

Please take a few minutes and be ready to organize and make practice announcements.

Questions Regarding Announcements

1. In the announcements, should the person say anything about late comers?

2. What if there are no announcements?

3. Who corrects the announcer?

4. Should there be a time limit on each announcement?

5. Should the announcements be made at the beginning or end of service?

6. What is the purpose of announcements?

7. Should additional announcements be solicited from the congregation?

8. Who filters the announcements? In other words, who decides what is retained or discarded?

Please lead a song.................. assign someone

Opening Pray....................………assign someone

Please make a five to ten-minute speech before or after class……......…………….. assign someone

Be ready to critique. Not criticize.

Lesson 3
Public Speaking

Whether you're a seasoned pro or giving a speech for the first time, the butterflies in your stomach always show up. As a seasoned pro, most individuals say they are still nervous.

For some, "Public Speaking" is not a gift that a person is born with. A presenter may feel some degree of nervousness before giving a public speech. Too much nervousness can be detrimental. Here are some tips on controlling the butterflies and presenting a great sermon/speech:

1. **Know your material.** Study and know more about your topic than you include in your speech. A presenter should use a degree of humor and personal stories to remember what they want to say.

2. **Practice. Practice. Practice!** Practice out loud. Use a timer and allow time for the unexpected.

3. **Know the audience.** Greet some as they arrive.

4. **Know the room.** A presenter should arrive early. A presenter should be familiar with the room.

5. **Watch yourself in the mirror.** Speak as if you are speaking to someone. To improve speaking ability, pay close attention to:

   - Your facial expressions
   - Your gestures
   - Your body movements.

   Realize and understand that people want you to be successful.

6. **Don't apologize for any nervousness or related problem(s).**

7. **Focus on the sermon/speech.**

Do's
1. Greet or welcome individuals.
2. Have a pleasant look.
3. Know your material.
4. Speak plainly.

Don'ts
5. Use excessive hand motions.
6. Be too relaxed.
7. Speak long.

Being a good public speaker will improve your reputation, boost your self-confidence, and open opportunities.
Remember, good public speaking can open doors; poor public speaking can close doors.

Questions Regarding Public Speaking

1. Should a speaker move around or stand still?

2. When a speaker notices that people in the audience are bored, what should the speaker do? Anything?

3. Does it mean anything if a speaker keeps saying "Um" and "Uh?"

4. If a speaker stands still, should they stand behind the lectern?

5. Can a speaker be too prepared?

6. Is there a difference between the body language of men and women?

7. What do you want the audience to say about you afterwards?

8. Which is more important—Content or Delivery?

Please lead a song.................. **assign someone**

Opening Pray..............…..………**assign someone**

Please make five to ten-minute speech before or after class………………………….. **assign someone**

Be ready to critique. Not criticize.

Lesson 4
Scripture Reading

The portion of scripture, the Old and New Testaments is the mind of God. The books are treasures. They contain the basic declarations concerning God and His children and the interrelationship between them. Throughout the book, especially the New Testament books, there is an appeal to believe and have faith in God the Eternal Father and in His Son.

The Word of God is the direct revelation of God to man. When a person reads it and obey it, it is beneficial and blessings will flow. It is God's chosen way to accomplish His divine will in the life of mankind. From the Mosaic dispensation to the Christian dispensation, God's Word has been and is communicated to His people through various forms. Reading scripture publically was a form of communicating God's will to His people.

When a person is reading scripture, he should keep in mind that the Word is sacred and powerful. It should be read in a translated version, not a paraphrased version.

This word is read out loud, typically on Wednesdays and Sundays to others. Some congregations meet on Thursday for Bible study and several scriptures are read. The reading should be conducted in such a way as to get God's message across to the listeners. Read as if the listeners are blind. Read naturally, be yourself and don't try to read like another person. To help, try reading in front of a mirror.

There are some do's and don'ts to consider when reading scripture publically:

Do's
1. Before reading the scriptures in front of an audience, it should be read at least three times, if possible.
2. When reading, stop at periods, pause at commas, and make questions sound like questions.
3. Give people an opportunity or time to find the scripture.
4. If the reader doesn't know the word, ask the speaker.
5. Leave comments to a minimum.

Don'ts

1. Read too fast or too slow.

Each scripture should be read in a maximum of two minutes. Practice reading the scriptures below:

> Matthew 5:1-11
> Hebrews 6:1-5
> I John 4:12-21
> I John 1:5-10
> Psalms 23 entire chapter
> Ecclesiastes 12:1-8
> Ephesians 6:10-18

Questions Regarding Scripture Reading

1. Should a woman be allowed to read? Why? or Why not?

2. Can a scripture reading be too long?

3. Should a Bible Interpretation or any Bible be used?

4. In the reading, if the reader does not punctuate or pronounce the scripture (s) correctly, should anything be said or done?

5. What is the significance of reading scripture?

6. Should additional passages be added or deleted in reference to scripture reading by the reader?

7. Is scripture powerful?

Please lead a song................. **assign someone**

Opening Prayer...............…........**assign someone**

Please make five to ten-minute speech before or after class regarding the Lord's Supper ....…... **assign someone**

Be ready to critique. Not criticize.

Lesson 5
Lord's Supper

The Lord's Supper or Communion is another part of worship that faithful individuals have an opportunity to participate in. When Paul wrote to the church in Corinth in II Corinthians 11:23-40, he stated that this was a remembrance of Christ and many were sick and dead because of the way they took it. Acts 20:7 lets us know they did partake on the first day of the week.

Make sure everything is ready before administering the Lord's Supper. That means making sure there's enough bread in the plates and enough fruit of the vine. Decide on and assign duties before surrounding the table.

Pray and serve the bread first. Then pray and serve the fruit of the vine. Please limit prayers to the bread and fruit of the vine only.

This is not a time for funny comments, comments about the sermon, or any other comments. When individuals administer the Lord's Supper, they should administer it in a way to help others remember Christ.

While serving, it is not a time to visit with friends and relatives. Do not rush anyone by handing the tray ahead of time or showing facial expressions. If you are serving, the tray should be given to members and non-members. Elderly members and non-members sitting at the beginning or end of the aisles should be assisted when possible.

We should ask the Lord to bless the bread and the wine, instead of saying "we" bless it. Also it is good to keep the prayers brief and not have a long pause when praying or speaking. Listed below are additional "do's and don'ts".

Do's
1. Distribute to everyone, Christians as well as non-Christians.
2. Make sure no one is omitted.
3. Go down the correct aisle.
4. Ask God to bless the bread and cup.

Don'ts
1. Force anyone.
2. Get confused.

The following scriptures that are used are
    Acts 20:7
    I Corinthians 11:23-34
    Matthew 26:26-30
    Luke 22:15-20
    I Corinthians 10:16-18
    Mark 14:22-26.

Questions Regarding Lord's Supper

1. Should brothers wear tee shirts and flip-flops while administering the Lord's Supper?

2. Should there be a song doing the Lord's Supper?

3. If the person administering the Lord's Supper is mistreating his wife or girlfriend after repenting four times earlier, should he continue to serve?

4. How should the Lord's Supper be handled on Sunday night? Should it be administered?

5. Will it be pleasing to the Lord if the Lord's supper is taken on the Sabbath?

6. What is transubstantiation?

7. Should we use one cup because of Matthew 26:27?

8. What's the purpose of the Lord's Supper?

9. If a person is in an incorrect position (instead of being on the end, they are in the center) around the table, should the person re-position themselves?

The few questions mentioned above will help the brothers be uniform or consistent when serving the Lord's Supper.

Please lead a song.................. **assign someone**

Opening Pray....................…...………**assign someone**

Please make five to ten-minute speech before or after class regarding Song Leading ……………
…………………………………………….. **assign someone**

Be ready to critique. Not criticize.

Lesson 6
Song Leading

Singing is a part of worship that is important, also. There is usually a male leading the congregation in song. If a brother is privileged to lead the congregation in song, there are a few things that need to be considered. He should

1. Be ready to lead, having songs picked out ahead of time

2. Select appropriate songs

3. Dress appropriately

4. Be enthusiastic.

If a person has to lead songs in worship, it should be taken seriously and not minimized. Leading God's people in song is a great honor. In smaller congregations, a single person may have to do everything. (I Peter 3:16)

Keep in mind, a person may lead the congregation in song, but everyone should be singing to God. God is the audience. Also, worshipping through songs sets the mood for other aspects of worship.

Do's
1. Sing familiar songs.
2. Lead songs; don't just listen.

Don'ts
1. Sing solo.

Leading God's people in song is not designed to make a person a song leader. If there is no desire to lead songs, show up to encourage those who try.

Later, there may be a workshop with a music teacher or a song leader to aid in reading notes, teaching music history, and adjusting vocals.

Questions Regarding Song Leading

1. Should the songs coincide with what's going on in the service? For example, if we are getting ready to serve the Lord's Supper, should a song be led that is about Christ's death, burial, or resurrection?

2. Is anything wrong with requesting a selection from the congregation?

3. Is it unscriptural to sing certain songs?

4. Is anything wrong with singing more songs than usual?

5. Is anything wrong with singing from a supplemental song book?

6. If a member feels uncomfortable singing a song, should they still lead the song?

7. Can any person lead songs?

8. What happens if the song leader starts singing solo?

9. In preparation for song leading, should songs be prepared ahead of time?

10. Is song leading important? If so, why?

Please lead a song.................. **assign someone**

Opening Pray..............................**assign someone**

Please make five to ten-minute speech before or after class regarding
Offering …........................….. **assign someone**

Be ready to critique. Not criticize.

Lesson 7
Offering

Most people will tell you, "I gave or I'm going to give 10% (tithe) to the Lord." Some people may not know where the 10% (tithe) came from.

Tithe is from the Hebrews "maaser" and the Greek "dekate" which means tenth. The Lord requires a tenth be given to Him in the Old Testament via the Levites. The first time we read of a tenth in the Bible is in Genesis 14:20. This is where Abram gave a tithe to Melchizedek. We are not commanded to tithe in the New Testament. We are commanded to give our offering to the Lord. Again, we don't tithe, we offer in the New Testament.

In reference to the offering, some will ask the question should I give from my net or gross? This question is not answered in scripture. A person should evaluate their love for the Lord and then use their discretion. Remember, "God loveth a cheerful giver." It's through the offerings:

- A church building is obtained.

- The gospel is shared in person, on the radio, and TV.
- Missionaries in and out of this country are supported.
- The local minister is supported.
- New sister congregations are assisted.
- Utilities are paid.
- Books, furniture, and communion ware are purchased.
- Ministries are funded.
- Those in need can receive assistance.
- Christians can fellowship.

Offering or giving is another aspect of worship. Many times the offering is implemented during the Lord's Supper or Communion.

We are stewards (Luke 12:15; Matthew 15:26). Being a steward means we realize that everything we have belongs to God and we should use it in a way pleasing unto Him.

Do's
1. Have collection envelopes available.
2. Have trays or pails available.

Don'ts
1. Deposit money in pockets because offering trays or pails are not available.
2. Go down incorrect aisle.

The below scriptures are usually used:
- I Corinthians 16:1-2
- II Corinthians 9:6-7

The instructor or teacher may want to explain the above scriptures in details.

Questions Regarding Offering

1. When a member stops and asks for change during the collection, what is the appropriate action to take?

2. Should a scripture be read before or during the offering?

3. Should a song be led during the offering?

4. If members are not giving, can anything be done or said? Example: There are 500 members and the collection is $3,000 dollars a week.

5. Is it appropriate to critique a brother on his prayer for the offering?

6. Why is it good to always have two brothers when handling the money?

7. Should prayer for the offering be initiated before or after the money is collected?

8. Should pledge cards or sheets be used?

Please lead a song.................. assign someone

Opening Pray...............…......…assign someone

Please make a five to ten-minute speech before or after class regarding Responses ....
...…................................…... assign someone

Be ready to critique. Not criticize.

Lesson 8
Responding to Reponses

Many congregations have a person to respond to individuals after the sermon has preached, whether it's for prayer or baptism. It is the responsibility of these people to respond to individuals.

The person should receive the comments from the individual or ask them privately. The information may be modified or deluded to be relayed to the congregation. Permission may have to be given regarding specific items. Then, the appropriate actions will be taken.

When the preacher finishes, a person should be in place and ready to take comments.

Do's
1. Show concern.

Don'ts
2. Minimize or disregard any comments.
3. Omit them in prayer.

Questions Regarding Responses to Responses

1. Should all responses (comments) from the person making the response be relayed to the congregation?

2. If someone is crying or is emotional should, anything be done to help them?

3. What if no one responds? Should prayer still be initiated?

4. What is the preferred method for responding, come up front, remain standing, or raise a hand?

5. If a person wants to respond but they don't, is it appropriate or okay to respond after service?

6. Should the person make their request out loud?

Please lead a song................. assign someone

Opening Pray..................………….assign someone

Please make five to ten-minute speech before or after class regarding Ushering .... ………………………………………….. **assign someone**

Be ready to critique. Not criticize.

Lesson 9
Ushering

Ushering is very important. The first person the visitors and/or guests meet is generally the usher. If a person has anything that has hindered their positive influence, THEY SHOULD NOT USHER. Some larger congregations will have greeters. For now, we are going to talk about small to medium congregations.

Some think that it is a minor task. There is more to ushering than opening the doors and leading someone to their seat. The usher controls the environment.

Illustration: The thermostat controls the temperature.

The usher is like a thermostat. He constantly monitors individuals. When a situation arises, it's the ushers who handle the situation in a way that's conducive, tactful, and diplomatic. If the ushers see several people fanning, the AC may need to be turned down. If individuals are shaking, the heat may need to be turned up.

Do's
1. Introduce yourself to a visitor or guest.
2. Be observant to various needs of members and non-members.
3. Assist members and non-members to their seats.
4. Try to sit visitors/guests by members.
5. Have two or more ushers on duty.
6. Make sure all visitors and guests have a visitor's card, bulletin, and a Bible.
7. Be alert. People may be there to do harm.

Don'ts
1. Point.
2. Leave assigned post without letting another usher know unless seating someone.
3. Seat or open a door for anyone during a prayer or communion.
4. Say the same thing to every person you meet.

An usher's duties are not finished after service, like many may believe. Ushers are responsible for picking-up and replacing hymnals, placing lost articles in a secure location, adjusting the heat or AC, and picking up paper or items to discard.

For a person to usher is a great privilege and honor (Psalm 84:10).

Questions Regarding Ushering

1. Should people be allowed to be seated anytime during service?

2. Can anyone be an usher?

3. How do you deal with unruly children?

4. Does an usher have ways to communicate with others, know the safest routes, and how to assist others that need help?

5. Should an usher know where to find the first-aid kits and/or the defibrillators?

6. How should safety issues be handled?

7. Should an usher be trained or know how to administer CPR?

8. How many ushers are needed on duty?

Please lead a song.................. assign someone

Opening Pray……….....………assign someone

Please make five to ten-minute speech before or after class regarding Baptism …………………. ………………………………….. assign someone

Be ready to critique. Not criticize.

Lesson 10
Baptizing

Jesus made a statement in Mark 16:16. It's apparent that He taught his disciples and they taught others. Baptizing is very important. Every person should know how to baptize and be prepared. The Bible says, "…be ready unto every good work…" (Titus 3:1).

If several people are seeking baptism, it's good to take the elderly or women first unless they specified differently.

The person being baptized should be given an opportunity to "confess" his or her belief in Christ. This may be done by asking the persons who come up front to be baptized, do they "believe that Jesus is the Christ, the Son of God"? This can also be done when the person is in the water and ready to be baptized.

Baptism is a burial, immersion, (Romans 6:4). The candidate must be baptized in water.

Some religious groups will perform baptisms once a month.

The Bible lets us know, through examples, commands, and inference that a person was baptized the same hour (Matthew 3:13-17; Acts 2:41; 8:29-38;16:33; Acts 19:1-5). The Bible also teaches that a person's sins are washed away.

In some congregations, songs are led while the person is preparing to be baptized. This is not required by scripture.

When a person is baptized, they are usually told to bend their knees, sit like they are sitting in a chair, put their left hand in the baptizer's right hand, and put their right hand over their nose. The baptizer should take them by the waist, place their hand in their back, and immerse them in the water slowly by taking them backward. The person being baptized should be told that the immersion will not take long. If the water is cold, the person should be warned.

Most baptizers will raise their right hand and say that they baptize that person in the name of the Father, the Son, and the Holy Ghost (Matthew 28:19) or in the name of Jesus (Acts 19:5). One of the following phrases is usually used:

> *In obedience to the commands of our Lord and Savior, Jesus Christ, you are now baptized for the remission of your sins in the name of the Father, the Son, and the Holy Spirit.*
>
> *I now baptize you in the name of the Father, Son, and the Holy Spirit for the remission of your sins.*

The baptizer should help the person out of the water, if possible and have a towel available for the baptized to dry off. It is good for the baptizer to have an extra shirt after the baptism, since their shirt may get soaked.

Do's
1. Make sure towels are available.
2. Make sure participants have clothing or a cap for their hair if they choose.
3. Make sure they make a confession.
4. Make sure they are assisted out of the water.
5. Give them a baptism certificate.

Don'ts
1. Cause the person to fear.
2. Discourage a person.

Baptism is a wonderful experience. Baptism identifies us with Christ's death on the cross, His burial in the tomb, and His resurrection from the dead. Baptism is a statement to everyone who witnesses it that the person has trusted Christ for his salvation and he's committed to living for Christ.

Questions Regarding Baptizing

1. Is it scriptural for a child to be baptized?

2. What's required for a person to be baptized?

3. Does a person need to be baptized with fire for their baptism to be acceptable in the Lord's sight?

4. Why was Jesus baptized?

5. Will sins be washed away in baptism?

6. What is the purpose of baptism?

7. Should there be a baptizer available after each sermon?

8. Should clothes and towels be available for the person being baptized?

9. Is saying the sinner's pray just as good as baptism?

10. Is anything wrong with being baptized twice?

11. Who is eligible to serve as a baptizer?

Please lead a song................... **assign someone**

Opening Pray..................………**assign someone**

Please make five to ten-minute speech before or after class regarding Teaching ………………… ……………………………………….. **assign someone**

Be ready to critique. Not criticize.

Lesson 11
Teaching

Teaching is a commandment that has been issued to everyone (Matthew 28:19-20). Teaching is a great privilege. A person is handling the Word of God. Below are ten things that a person should implement to become a good teacher.

One. To be a good teacher, a person must desire or have great passion about what they are doing. They must be able to motivate others to learn and teach them how to learn.

Two. Teaching is about pushing people to do their best. It also means giving your best.

Three. Teaching is being like Christ by motivating others to excel, communicating with them, and respecting them.

Four. It make no difference if you end up with a small

number of students. As long as you can inspire others and feel good about your efforts, it's alright.

Five. To be a good teacher is working the room and helping students realize they have great potential.

Six. To be a good teacher, relax and let students know being human means making mistakes but not giving up. Keep on keeping on.

Seven. Good teaching is about devoting time.

Eight. Good teaching is reflected in what is said and done.

Nine. Good teaching is about mentoring. It's also about recognizing and rewarding others.

Ten. Good teachers teach because they love it, not because they have to put up with knock heads. They do it because they want to.

Questions Regarding Teaching

1. With men and women in an adult class, is anything wrong with a woman teaching the class?

2. Should a nursery class be available? Why? Or why not?

3. Does it matter if an objective is given to individuals for the class?

4. How is the subject or the material for the classes determined?

5. What is the process for a person to be able to teach?

6. How is a student assigned to a particular class?

7. When does a student move on to a different class?

8. Does it mean anything when a person is not talkative in class?

9. Are there any warning signs for a troubled person in class?

*M*oses

(Exodus 3, Numbers, Leviticus, Deuteronomy)

Moses (Hebrew: מֹשֶׁה, Standard Moshe Tiberian Mōšeh (7 Adar 2368 - 7 Adar 2488 in the Hebrew calendar; 1393 - 1273 BCE); Arabic: موسى, Mūsa; Ge'ez: ሙሴ Musse) was an early Biblical Hebrew lawgiver via God, prophet, and to whom the authorship of the Torah is traditionally attributed. Moses means "The one drawn out" (Ex. 2:10).

The Book of Exodus started many years after the Book of Genesis ended, the Israelites were dwelling in harmony with the Egyptians in the Land of Goshen, the eastern part of the Nile Delta.

After the king of Egypt died, another king was appointed and was hostile to the Israelites and enslaved them. After a period of time had passed, Moses killed an Egyptian slave master (Exodus 2:11-12) after he saw the slave master smiting (hitting) his Hebrew brother.

Pharaoh, the king, found out, and wanted to kill Moses, but Moses ran away to the land of Midian where he raised sheep for forty years. (Exodus 2:15; Acts 7:28-30). While in Midian, he saw a burning bush that was not consumed by the fire. The Bible says Moses turned aside to see this great wonder. It was at this point that God called Moses from the burning bush to lead the children of Israel out of Egyptian bondage.

God through Moses unleashed ten plagues on Egypt. After unleashing the last plague, Pharaoh released the Hebrew slaves. Moses led the Hebrew slaves to the Red Sea. When they were trapped, Moses said, "Fear ye not, stand still, and see the salvation of the Lord..." To make a long story short, Moses led the children of Israel through the Red Sea. Afterwards they wondered in the wilderness 40 years because of disobedience. Consider these three points before answering the below questions:

- God's Presence
- God's Program
- God's Person.

God promised to be with Moses. God revealed what He was going to do and God used the person of Moses to accomplish His program.

1. If God promises to be with us today, (Hebrew 13:5) like he was with Moses (Exodus 3:12) why is there doubt when we have a Red Sea experience?

2. Moses used five excuses for God not to use Him, "Who am I (vs.11), what shall I say unto them (Vs. 13), they will not believe me (Ex. 4:1), I am slow of speech and of a slow tongue (Ex. 4:10), send someone else" (Ex 4:13). Do we use excuses for not wanting to lead God's people? Please explain. What are some of the excuses we use?

3. Moses herded sheep, and it is said he led over a million people. Is there any lesson that can be learned from Moses concerning leadership?

4. In Numbers 20, Moses led the children of Israel through the wilderness. Moses struck the rock instead of speaking to it as God had commanded. Because of that, Moses was not permitted to go into the Promised Land. What characteristic(s) did Moses lack concerning the children of Israel? Do we lack similar characteristic(s) today in leading God's people? Please explain.

5. Moses led and judged the people. Is it appropriate to judge people as leaders today?

6. God, through Moses, provided the children of Israel with protection, food and clothing (Deuteronomy 29:5). Are we required to provide anything to God's people today besides the Word?

*J*oshua
(Joshua)

Joshua, **Jehoshuah**, or **Yehoshua** (Hebrew: יְהוֹשֻׁעַ, Tiberian: jə.hoˈʃuaʕ, Israeli: Yəhoshúa), born in Egypt, was an Israelite leader who was the assistant and successor of Moses. His name means "Jehovah saves." He was one of the 12 spies sent by Moses to spy out the land of Canaan.

Joshua was a servant (Exodus 24:13; Numbers 13:16) and a soldier (Exodus 17:8-16). He led the children of Israel into the promised land. Joshua conquered Jericho but suffered a defeat at Ai because of sin in the camp. After correcting the sin problem, he was successful in conquering all his enemies.

1. What lessons can we learn about Joshua being a servant and a soldier first before he led the child of Israel?

2. Is it possible for one sin by an individual cause problems in the congregation, like Achan's sin caused in the camp? Please explain.

3. In Joshua 1, God commanded Joshua to follow some principles to be successful. What are the principles? Will those same principles guarantee success for us today?

4. In Joshua 6:3-5, the Lord commanded Joshua to march around the city once a day for six days, followed by seven priests walking ahead of the Ark and marching around the city seven times on the seventh day, then shout with a great shout. As you know, the walls came tumbling down. What's required as a leader to make (not only ours but others) our walls (problems, difficulties, despair) come tumbling down?

5. In Numbers 13, Moses sent out 12 spies to spy on the land of Canaan. Joshua and Caleb were the only two who came back with a positive report, indicating they were able to overcome their enemy. Can any lessons be learned?

Gideon
(Judges 6)

Gideon **Gideon**, KJV of NT **Gedeon**. [Heb. *Gidon*, "hewer, feller or great warrior;" Gr. *Gedeon*.] Gideon was a judge and a deliverer of the Hebrews. He was the son of Joash, the Abiezrite (Judges 6:11). His name was changed to Jerubbaal (Judges 6:32), which means in the Hebrew, *Yerubbaal*, which means "let Baal contend against him."

Because of disobedience (sin) by the children of Israel, God sent the Midianites in multitude to oppress the Israelites for seven years. During this time, the children of Israel were crying out for help against the Midianites.

Gideon was called by an angel of the Lord while threshing wheat in the wine press at Ophrah to hide his harvest from the Midianites (Judges 6:11). Gideon started out with 32,000 to fight against the Midianites and ended up with 300 per God's instructions. He led 300 against the Midianites and was called by an angel of the Lord to deliver Israel.

1. Gideon did not refuse the call of God to lead the children of Israel out of oppression. Why do people refuse God in leading people out of bondage now? Please explain.

2. God used the Midianites to oppress the children of Israel because of sin. When we go through difficulties and problems in our lives, is it because of sin? Please explain.

3. Gideon started out with a large number to fight against the Midianites and ended up with a much smaller number. Are there any lessons for us to learn?

4. In Judges 6:25-32, Gideon destroyed the altar of Baal. Why did Gideon destroy the altar of Baal? Why don't we destroy or speak against what we consider false worship today?

5. In Judges 6:36-40, Gideon asked for signs from God to lead an attack against the Midianites. Should we seek a sign from God to lead a person out of sin?

*D*avid

(1 & 2 Samuel, 1 & 2 Kings, 1 & 2 Chronicles, Psalms, Proverbs)

David **David**. Heb. *Dawid*, usually interpreted to mean "beloved." The son of Jesse the Bethlehermite, the youngest of seven bothers (I Samuel 16:10-13), was born in Bethlehem (I Samuel 16:1). David was the second king of Israel.

1. I Samuel 17 talks about David defeating Goliath. Saul, the first king of Israel, and the soldiers, ran from Goliath because they were scared (I Samuel 17:11, Psalm 8). Do we run from problems that seem to be impossible to defeat? Why?

2. In I Samuel 18:6-16, Saul, the first king, becomes jealous of David. How do we overcome our jealousy of someone who has abilities greater than ours?

3. In I Samuel 24 & I Samuel 26, David DID NOT kill King Saul when given an opportunity. What lesson(s) can we learn?

4. In I Samuel 28:3-25, why did King Saul want to raise Samuel from the dead?

5. I Chronicles 13 talks about David consulting with captains and leaders about moving the Ark of God and one man (Uzza) lost his life. Is it possible to lose one's life today because of bad advice or bad spiritual decisions?

6. II Samuel 11 talks about the story of David and Bathsheba and how David conspired to kill Bathsheba's husband. Is it possible to commit murder and not be conscious of it today?

7. II Samuel 12 is the story of Nathan the prophet going to David to remind him of what David has done. Does God send people in our lives to inform us of things that we otherwise are unaware of?

8. In I Samuel 18:1-5, I Samuel 20, David and Jonathan become very close friends. Are there any lesson(s) we can learn about friendship?

9. Acts 13:22 says that David was a man after God's own heart. I Samuel 13:14 talks about God looking for a man after his own heart. What does, "David was a man after God's own heart" actually mean?

10. In II Samuel 9, Jonathan's lame son, Mephibosheth was allowed to eat at David's table. Because of Christ, God allows us at His table in spite of our lame condition. Are we seated at the Lord's Table? If not, why not?

Elijah
(I & II Kings)

Elijah, [Heb. "my God is Jehovah"]. Elijah was a prophet of God (I Kings 19:14). He was a Tishbite from Gilead. Elijah exhibits courage when confronting King Ahab.

1. I Kings 17:1 and James 5:17 let us know that Elijah prayed that it would not rain for three and a half years. If prayer is so powerful, why don't we pray more today?

2. King Ahab was a bad king in I Kings 18:1-19 and he is confronted. Should we as Christians confront one another when we backslide or start doing sinful things?

3. Please read I Kings 18:19-40 about Elijah at Mount Carmel. Please share any practical lesson(s) from the story.

4. In I Kings 19:19-21, Elijah called Elisha. How does this apply to us today?

5. In II Kings 2:1-11, Elijah was taken up in a whirlwind by God. God functioned in a supernatural way. Elijah had successfully completed his mission on earth. What hinders us from completing our mission today?

Solomon

(II Samuel 12:24-25, I Kings, II Chronicles, Psalm 72,127, Songs of Solomon)

Solomon (so¬l'o\®-mu¬n). [Heb. Shelomoh, "peaceable He was the son of David and Bathsheba (2 Samuel 12:24; 1 Chronicle 3:5). Solomon was the third and last king of Israel. He also was called Jedidiah, "beloved of Yahweh" in 2 Samuel 12:25.

1. In I Kings 3:3-15, Solomon asked for wisdom to lead God's people. What is wisdom and do we need wisdom today to lead God's people?

2. I Kings 3:16-28 talks about an example of Solomon's wisdom and the love of a mother. Solomon judged these two harlots (prostitutes) that demonstrated his wisdom. As a leader, how can wisdom be demonstrated?

3. In I Kings 6, Solomon begins to build the temple (church) with his Father's help. Will God help today in building the church? Think about your answer before responding.

4. Solomon did evil in the Lord's sight (verse 6). When a person does evil in the Lord's sight, what should they do?

5. I Kings 11:1-8, Solomon married 700 wives and obtained 300 concubines, which turned his heart away from God (verse 4). Even though it's wrong to have more than one spouse today, is it possible to allow our hearts to be turned aside from the true and living God by a spouse?

6. How did God punish Solomon for sinning? What lessons can we learn from this?

7. Are there any lessons we can learn from Solomon, who "turned away after other gods"?

8. I Kings 12:1-20 talks about the Northern Tribe revolting against Solomon's son, Rehoboam. Why did the tribes revolt?

9. Why do people revolt on the Lord today? Is there any way to stop them? Please explain.

*I*saiah

(Isaiah 1-66, II Chronicles 32, II Kings 19-21)

Isaiah the son of Amoz (Isaiah 38:1). He was a prophet (II Kings 19:2). The meaning of his name is "God is salvation." The book of Isaiah is referred to the most in the New Testament.

1. In Isaiah 7:1-12, God sent Isaiah to reassure King Ahaz of victory over his enemies. Does God assure us of victory today?

2. In II Kings 19, Isaiah and Hezekiah ask God for help. God sent an angel that destroyed 185,000 Assyrian troops. Is it right to ask God for help in destroying people now?

3. In II Kings 20, God, through the prophet Isaiah, told Hezekiah to set his house in order because he was going to die. Do we have a chance to set our house in order before we die? Please explain.

4. God spared Hezekiah's life and added 15 years to his life because he prayed to God. Are there any lessons to learn from Hezekiah?

5. Isaiah was a prophet of God to deliver messages to the King and the children of Israel. What message should we be delivering to others?

Jeremiah
(Jeremiah)

Jeremiah was the son of Hilkuah, currently living in Anathoth in the land of Benjamin (Jeremiah 1:1). His name means "whom Jehovah has appointed." Jeremiah is also called "the Weeping Prophet."

1. The nation of Israel sinned against God by worshipping false gods and forgetting the true God. Can we do anything to remind people of God?

2. Can we do anything to remind people of true worship?

3. In Jeremiah 7, the people were causing their "sons and daughters to pass through the fire" which the Lord did not command. In other words, they were sacrificing their sons and daughters in the fire. What sacrifices should we offer to the Lord today?

4. Jeremiah was called "the Weeping Prophet." He was distressed both by the disobedience and apostasy of Israel. Should we be disturbed because of disobedience and sin in others lives?

5. In Jeremiah 26:6-9; 28; 37:11-21; 38:1-13, Jeremiah was persecuted severely. What is persecution and do we suffer any today?

6. Jeremiah 31: 31-34 talks about a New Covenant. What is this New Covenant that Jeremiah is making reference to?

Ezekiel
(Ezekiel)

Ezekiel (Yehezkel in Hebrew) was a priest. He was the son of Buzi, in the land of the Chaldeans by the river Chebar (Ezekiel 1:1-3). The meaning of his name is "God is Strong."

1. In Ezekiel 5, Ezekiel cut his hair for a sign. Are there any outward signs evident that we are Christians?

2. Ezekiel was a man of God that condemned Jerusalem by the Word of God. Are we condemned today by God's Word?

3. In Ezekiel 18, God through Ezekiel said "…the soul that sinneth, it shall die." How can the soul sinneth?

4. Judah and Jerusalem would not repent because of the disobedience and sin they committed, God sent their enemies to destroy them as punishment. When we fail to repent, does God send others to punish us?

5. How does the disobedience of children of Israel make reference to leadership?

6. What was to be offered as a sin offering for the priests and Levites? (Leviticus 43:18-26)

Daniel
(Daniel)

Daniel. [Heb. and Aramaic *Danéyel*]. The latter form means, "my God is judge."

1. Daniel, along with some Hebrew boys, was selected by King Nebuchadnezzar to perform service unto him. Daniel determined not to defile himself with the king's meat. So, he made a proposal that they eat vegetables and drink water for ten days, then compare them with people that had eaten from the king's table (Daniel 1:1-14). Are there any lesson(s) we can learn from this story?

2. Daniel 5 talks about the king making a great feast and mysterious handwriting on a wall. Sometimes, other people cannot tell you what God's will is for your life. God may allow you to consume food in fellowshipping. You may not receive a mysterious handwriting, but does God warns us of impeding danger?

3. In Daniel 6, Daniel was thrown in a lion's den because he would not worship a false god. The Bible teaches us that in spite of the decree, he prayed three times a day to his God (verse 10). Are there any lessons to learn from this?

4. What characteristics of a leader did Daniel have that people need today?

5. In Daniel 9, he prays for the people. Why is praying for others a good quality of a leader?

Jesus Christ
(Matthew, Mark, Luke, John)

Jesus Christ Heb. "Joshua," meaning "Yahweh is salvation." Christos Heb. "Messiah," meaning "anointed," or "anointed one." The Savior of the world, the Messiah.

1. Jesus was sent to carry out the Father's will. What is His will for our lives?

2. In Matthew 4, Christ was tempted by Satan in the wilderness after fasting forty days and forty nights. Christ overcame Satan by quoting the Word. When tempted by Satan, what should we do besides quote the Word?

3. Jesus gave a parable in Luke 12:13-21, the Prosperous Farm. What is the primary point?

4. Jesus healed a man in Bethsaida that was born blind. What lesson(s) can we learn from this story?

5. In John 11, Jesus raised Lazarus from the dead. Does Jesus raise us from the dead today? If so, how?

6. When Jesus was crucified, He asked the Father to forgive them. What lesson(s) can we learn?

7. In John 20:24-29, Thomas was not there for Jesus' first appearing. Is it possible to miss Jesus?

8. In John 6, many followed Jesus for the wrong reasons. Can you detect when a person is not following Jesus for the right reason?

Paul

(Acts, Romans, Galatians, Ephesians, Philippians, Colossians, I & II Corinthians, I & II Thessalonians, I & II Timothy, Titus, Philemon)

Paul was born and raised in Tarsus in Ciltca (Acts 21:39). He was of the tribe of Benjamin (Romans 11:1). Paul was a Hebrew of Hebrews (Philippians 3:5). Educated at the feet of Gamaliel (Acts 22:3). A son of a Pharisee (Acts 23:6). He persecuted Christians (Galatians 1:13, Acts 26:10, Acts 22:5.19, & Acts 8:3.

1. In Acts 9:1-19, Saul (Paul) was on his way to Damascus to throw Christians in jail. The Lord knocked him down on his way to Damascus and asked him a question, "…why persecutest thou me?" How is it possible to persecute the Lord by persecuting other Christians?

2. Does the Lord have to knock us down, like Saul (Paul), to get our attention?

3. When the Lord called Saul (Paul), he did not delay (Galatians 1:11-24). Why do people delay God's call today?

4. In Acts 16:16-40, Paul (Saul) and Silas were thrown in prison for casting out a spirit in a demon possessed girl. Are there demons today and do we have the power to cast them out of people today?

5. In Romans 8:31, Paul said, "If God be for us, who can be against us?" What does this statement mean and does it apply to Christians today?

Peter
(Acts, I & II Peter)

Peter. Greek - Petros, "stone," a translation of the Aramaic Kepha, "Cephas," "rock," or "stone." See John 1:42. One of the Twelve, also called Simon. Greek - Simoμn and Sumeoμn, from Hebrew Shimon, "Simeon".

Peter's father is named Jonah (John 1:42). Peter preached the first gospel sermon and about 3,000 souls were baptized for the remission of their sins (Acts 2:14-42). Peter denied the Lord three times (Matthew 26:31-75, Mark 27-72, Luke 22:31-62, John 13:36-38, 18:15-18).

1. In Matthew 14:28-29, Peter took one step off the boat from the natural to the supernatural. Can we make that step today?

2. Many followed Peter hoping that his shadow might overshadow them (Acts 5:15). What's needed to happen to have many follow you like they followed Peter?

3. In Acts 3:1-10, Peter and John healed a lame man that was at the temple gate. For all practical purposes, this man was at the door of church. Would you help a person at the door of the church asking for help? Why or why not?

4. In Matthew 26:36-46, Mark 14:32-42, Luke 22:39-46, Jesus took Peter and others disciples with Him to Gethsemane for prayer before his crucifixion. But the Bible tells us that they feel asleep three times. Do we fall asleep on Jesus today?

5. In Acts 5:1-11, Peter told Ananias and Sapphira that they had conspired to lie to the Lord about selling property and because of that, they fell dead. Are there any lesson(s) to learn from this story?

www.ingramcontent.com/pod-product-compliance
Lightning Source LLC
Chambersburg PA
CBHW050446010526
44118CB00013B/1696